November
2021

Viz Zeller

Chapter 7 Best

Lots of Edgar Cayce Readings

The Essenes
AND THE ADVENT OF JESUS

A study guide for the Advent season based on the Holy Bible and Edgar Cayce Readings

JEFFREY IMES

The Essenes and the Advent of Jesus

ISBN: 978-1-09839-353-3

For to us a child is born, to us a son is given, and the government will be on his shoulders. And he will be called

Wonderful Counselor,
Mighty God,
Everlasting Father,
Prince of Peace.

Of the increase of his government and peace there will be no end. He will reign on David's throne and over his kingdom, establishing and upholding it with justice and righteousness from that time on and forever. The zeal of the LORD Almighty will accomplish this.

(Isaiah 9:6–7 NIV)

CONTENTS

PREFACE

The Christmas season is filled with life-sized and miniature scenes depicting the baby Jesus lying in a manger surrounded by adoring parents, shepherds, and wise men. Church plays performed by excited and nervous children reenact the birth of the Messiah and Savior of mankind to a young girl named Mary. Children in robes depict the lowly shepherds and educated wise men paying homage to Mary and the newborn Messiah.

Mary has embarked on this miraculous journey because the angel Gabriel appeared to her and announced that she had been chosen by God, because of her purity and righteousness, to be the mother of His son. Pastors and priests compose sermons woven around the Advent story, integrating scripture readings and church traditions to recount the events leading to the birth of the baby Jesus and his future role as the Messiah. The Advent story unfolds in churches the world over during the few weeks leading to the birth of Jesus on Christmas day.

How much of the traditional Christmas story told in pulpits and Sunday school classes today is authentic and factual, and how much is extrapolation and embellishment of the few Bible verses that portray the events leading to and surrounding the birth of Jesus? No Bible verses describe the childhood and life circumstances of Mary in the years preceding her choice as the mother of the Messiah, and so we are not given insight into the personal qualities that caused God to favor her over other possible choices. Nor are we told why God chose that particular time and place to send His Son into the world. Bible verses that describe the manner in which she was chosen are sparse and contain few details other than Gabriel's attempt to allay her fears and give her reassurance that she can bear the Messiah even though she is still a virgin.

The Advent message and Christmas story we hear and accept today is a traditional interpretation of these verses that have their origins in the fourth century more than three hundred years after the birth of Jesus and have evolved since then. In these lessons, we will take a fresh look at the Advent story as constructed from a combination of information from the readings of Edgar Cayce and biblical text. The Cayce readings do not contradict the biblical account of events leading to the birth of Jesus, but they do add considerable background material covering the years before His birth, fill in some of the gaps in the biblical material, and correct some apparent misperceptions prevalent in the traditional interpretation of those biblical verses.

The readings tell of individuals who dedicated their lives to God and were active within a community that was established and existed for the purpose of making it possible for the Messiah to enter the earth. The foundation of that community was in place at least four hundred years before Jesus was born. By the time of Jesus, it was known as the Essenes, meaning "Expectancy," which expresses the anticipation and hope they felt as they prepared themselves for the long-awaited event.

It is clear that the birth of Jesus was preceded by and required the dedication and active participation of many persons.

These persons were more than just passive bystanders to a miraculous event orchestrated by God; they were participants in the event, willingly becoming the hands and feet of God, the channels through which God's purpose and plan for mankind was to be fulfilled. Despite all they had seen and done, even the Essenes may not have fully realized that Jesus would be the living example of the ideal relationship between God and man, and that he would teach the Way and the Truth that has the power to free man from his self-inflicted separation from God and reunite his soul with its Creator.

1
COERCION OR CALLING

In the sixth month, God sent the angel Gabriel to Nazareth, a town in Galilee, to a virgin pledged to be married to a man named Joseph, a descendant of David.

The virgin's name was Mary. The angel went to her and said, "Greetings, you who are highly favored! The Lord is with you." Mary was greatly troubled at his words and wondered what kind of greeting this might be.

But the angel said to her, "Do not be afraid, Mary, you have found favor with God. You will be with child and give birth to a son, and you are to give him the name Jesus. He will be great and will be called the Son of the Most High.

The Lord God will give him the throne of his father David, and he will reign over the house of Jacob forever; his kingdom will never end."

"How will this be," Mary asked the angel, "since I am a virgin?" The angel answered, "The Holy Spirit will come upon you, and the power of the Most High will overshadow you. So the holy one to be born will be called the Son of God.

*Even Elizabeth your relative is going to have a child in
her old age, and she who was said to be barren is in
her sixth month. For nothing is impossible with God."
"I am the Lord's servant," Mary answered. "May it be
to me as you have said." Then the angel left her.*

(Luke 1:26-38 NIV)

*This is how the birth of Jesus Christ came about: His
mother Mary was pledged to be married to Joseph, but
before they came together, she was found to be with
child through the Holy Spirit.*

*Because Joseph her husband was a righteous man and
did not want to expose her to public disgrace, he had
in mind to divorce her quietly.*

(Matthew 1:18-19 NIV)

The common interpretation of the few biblical verses in
Luke that describe the visit of the angel Gabriel to Mary and her
response to his announcement that she would be the mother of
Jesus includes the assumption that Mary was a young pious village girl worthy of the honor and chosen by God without her
prior knowledge. She was blindsided by the announcement, but
handled it with poise and decorum. In Luke 1:34 she responds to
the announcement by asking how she can have a child when she
is a virgin.

Since Mary was already betrothed to Joseph (Luke1:27)
before the vision and announcement, wouldn't a more natural

response be for her to assume that she would give birth to this special child after she was married and had sexual relationships with her husband? Why would she assume that she had to become pregnant or give birth to the child before her marriage?

Does this indicate some confusion and fluster on her part as she attempted to make sense of the sudden and unexpected proclamation? Abraham faced a similar situation. When he was told by God that his wife Sarai would have a child, he immediately assumed that it would occur by normal birth and questioned God's word because it seemed physically impossible to him (Gen 17:15–17).

The reaction of Mary (Luke1:38) to the announcement seems more like resigned acceptance rather than enthusiastic joy. Nevertheless, she is recorded as having believed and accepted the vision and concludes that her pregnancy will begin before she is married to Joseph. Gabriel confirms her conclusion and describes the manner in which she will become pregnant and the fact that her child will be the Son of God.

When Joseph hears that Mary has become pregnant before their marriage he reacts with considerable dismay and apprehension, and he wrestles with the unpleasant fact before finally coming to terms with it after receiving assurance and guidance from the angel Gabriel.

In this traditional view, Mary apparently had no inkling before the vision that she would become pregnant by the Holy Spirit without having known a man. She apparently had no mental or physical preparation for the angelic announcement which could have caused serious emotional stress to any unprepared peasant girl. She probably had no real concept of the affect and influence her son would have on the Jewish nation and the history of mankind even though Gabriel described him as the Son of God. Under the circumstances, that description of the child would likely bring to her attention the nature of the conception, not the future possibilities of the child.

Imagine the effect of this pronouncement on Mary. She was a normal young teenager, of marriageable age for girls in that society at that time, but the suddenness of the announcement would have been shocking and the dawning awareness of the impact it would have on her life surely must have been difficult to accept.

Imagine the effect of this event on her relationship with her parents. That relationship surely would have undergone a radical change for the worse as she tried to explain her unexpected and indefensible pregnancy. Would her protestations and pleading have been sufficient to convince her parents that she was pregnant by God, and not her future husband or a local village boy? Would she consider and fear the possibility of honor killing, the strict code still illicitly practiced in some Middle Eastern countries today, whereby a family believes it redeems its honor and saves face by murdering an offending family member who has broken tradition or religious law?

Imagine the effect of her pregnancy on her standing in the community and the likely deterioration of her relationships with village adults and friends. Isn't it possible that she (and perhaps her family) would become an outcast in her own village as the pregnancy became apparent to the community elders? Village neighbors and even friends might have condemned and ostracized her, and perhaps even attempted to have her stoned to death for adultery.

The society of Mary's day was not tolerant of women who had children out of wedlock. It seems unlikely that they would rally around her and praise her for carrying God's child simply on the basis of her word. The village and home environment would not have been conducive to the rearing of any child with the stigma of illegitimacy, and certainly would not be a loving environment for the Son of God.

Even if the teenage Mary could and did quickly come to terms with God's decision, the initial shock would surely have been nearly overwhelming. Without a support group of friends and mentors who also were aware of the unique manner of conception, all of the weight of that reality would fall on her shoulders. It is easy to say that God was with her, so she could endure any abuse or ill feeling, but why would God forcibly place her and His Son in that situation?

What happened to Mary's free will and right to make her own choices? Is her apparent lack of choice in the matter incompatible with the free will decision of Jesus in the Garden of Gethsemane many years later? Jesus would struggle with the knowledge of the pain, suffering and humiliation He would have to endure if He chose to follow God's plan to its conclusion. But He still retained the opportunity to choose to accept God's will for His life, which would lead to the cross, or to reject God's will and follow His own sense of self preservation.

The mental anguish He went through clearly shows that the decision was not easy even for the Son of God. It was only because He willingly permitted his capture by the Jewish religious authorities and submitted to the interrogations and torture of the Jews and Roman civil authority that He was crucified. Why do we praise Jesus for His courageous choice and selfless act, and never consider that tradition denies Mary the same choice about how her body would be used. We simply accept that it was her assigned role to be the mother of God's Son because it suited God's purpose.

So, how does one reconcile the common interpretation of the biblical verses that record the choosing of Mary as the mother of the Messiah with the apparent violation of her free will and the almost certain negative personal and social consequences to Mary within her family and among the members of their local community. The readings present an alternative interpretation and description of these events that is consistent with the biblical verses, but more comprehensive and richer in detail, and more acceptable than the traditional interpretation of the biblical text.

The entrance of the Messiah into the material world did not and could not begin by the coerced conception of a village teenager, no matter how pious she may have been and how willingly she may have accepted the news. Before Mary was born, it was already her soul's decision and spiritual purpose to present herself as a candidate for the role of mother of the Messiah. That spiritual purpose became crystallized and manifested in the physical world as she was offered and accepted that role, and when she willingly embraced the demands that would be placed upon her mind and body. She, like Jesus, made a choice.

QUESTIONS TO PONDER

1. Does the traditional interpretation of biblical verses that describe the choosing of Mary suggest an arbitrary and dictatorial God who disrespects the free will He already has granted us? Or does the magnitude and meaning of the story of Jesus override any objections you might have of a possible intrusion upon Mary's individuality and free will?

2. Does God impose His will on us to make sure we act according to His desire or to fulfill his purposes, or does God place situations and opportunities before us that can lead to a closer relationship with Him if we make the correct life choices? Which option is more likely to cause the soul to spiritually advance and become more conscious of its creator? How do we ensure that our freely-made choices will cause our will to be better aligned with His will and allow us to better manifest His purposes in the earth?

3. At the Garden of Gethsemane, Jesus willingly made the choice to give up His physical life so that the rest of mankind would have evidence that the way He taught not only leads to a moral and spiritual earthly life, but also to eternal life and companionship with God. Would

the sacrifice of Jesus have the same meaning and value to us if He had simply received an order from God stating that He was to be sacrificed on a cross? As Christians, are we required daily to make the same kinds of decisions that Jesus made? Don't we always have the option of taking the easy path defined by our selfish interests as opposed to taking the more difficult path that comes from sacrificing our selfishness and seeking to glorify God in our words and actions?

4. Can you recall any situation in the Old or New Testament where God forced His will on any person? Jonah and Paul may come to mind. How do their experiences differ from that of the traditional account of Mary? Were they denied their free will or were they faced with the consequences of their previous actions and offered an alternate path? When a person uses his free will to direct evil actions toward another person, do we have the right and duty to prevent that action even though we violate his free will?

2
THE SCHOOL OF PROPHETS AND THE ESSENES

From whence arose the purpose of idea or ideal that ye hold so close in thine experience? YE say that there were those periods when for four hundred years little or nothing had happened in the experience of man as a revelation from the Father, or from God, or from the sources of light.

WHAT was it, then, that made the setting for the place and for the entering in of that consciousness into the earth that YE know as the Son of man, the Jesus of Nazareth, the Christ on the Cross?

Did the darkness bring the light? Did the wandering away from the thought of such bring the Christ into the earth? Is this idea not rather refuting the common law that is present in spirit, mind and body that "Like begets like?"

[Edgar Cayce Reading 262-61]

As was asked oft, "Can any good thing come out of Nazareth?" Isn't it rather that there were those, that ye hear little or nothing of in thine studies of same, that dedicated their lives, their minds, their bodies, to a purpose, to a SEEKING for that which had been

*to them a promise of old? Were there not individuals,
men and women, who dedicated their bodies that they
might be channels through which such an influence,
such a BODY might come?*

[Edgar Cayce Reading 262-61]

The Bible is silent about God's activity in the earth during
the four hundred or more years between the predictions of the
Old Testament prophets Isaiah (Isa. 7:14 and Isa. 9:6) and Micah
(Micah 5:2) about the coming of a Messiah and the birth of Jesus.
Does this mean that during this long period of history God was
no longer working through prophets and spiritually-minded people to bring a message of hope to a lost world? Was this a time of
complete spiritual darkness when God stepped aside and left the
world to itself?

When the source of reading 262-61 presented the question,
"Did the wandering away from the thought of such [the promised
Messiah] bring the Christ into the earth?" he did more than simply imply that the events leading up to and surrounding the birth
of Jesus did not unfold in an arbitrary manner in the absence of
God's activity in the earth or without men actively seeking and
facilitating the promised event. He also conveyed the idea that the
birth of the Messiah without intentional activity directed toward
the accomplishment of that event would violate a spiritual law
described as "like begets like." This law means that events and situations in the material world are causal and are influenced by the
spiritual awareness and maturity of the participants.

The readings refer to this long period of time, about which the Bible has nothing to say, by posing the interesting questions, "Did the darkness bring the light? Did the wandering away from the thought of such bring the Christ into the earth?" These questions are asking if the Light of Christ that would fill the world as a result of the birth of Jesus could spring from a four-hundred-year spiritual drought and period of spiritual darkness in the earth. The questions were crafted to emphasize that such a momentous spiritual event as the birth of the Messiah required the dedication, commitment, and preparation of many individuals, and that the four-hundred-year gap in the biblical record was not a time of spiritual inactivity but a time of spiritual preparation focused on and leading to the birth of Jesus. Because that activity is not recorded in the Bible does not mean it did not occur.

The story of the birth of Jesus starts not with the visitation of the angel Gabriel to Mary, but with the preparations of a group of dedicated people within the Jewish Essene community centered around Mount Carmel who set themselves aside from the greater Jewish society in spirit and action, believing that the long-promised Messiah would be born in their midst. The readings clearly suggest that the Messiah would not and could not enter the earth and accomplish his purpose unless a sufficient number of individuals were dedicated to that purpose and acted in a manner to open the way and facilitate the event. With their lives dedicated to God, the Essenes would manifest in the earth "the setting for the place and for the entering of that consciousness into the earth that ye know as the Son of man, Jesus of Nazareth, the Christ on the Cross".

God promised Lot that the destruction of Sodom could be turned aside by the actions and prayers of just ten righteous men (Gen 18:23–32). The future physical destruction of a city, a consequence of the sinful nature and activity of its residents, could be turn aside by the concerted actions of a few faithful citizens. In the same manner, the willingness of the members of the Essene community and their predecessors to act in a cooperative manner for a higher spiritual cause changed the course of history and brought forth the means of spiritual salvation for a sinful world.

The righteous actions of a dedicated minority of citizens can provide new opportunities for the sinful majority to repair their relationship with God and alter their destiny. Apparently, ten righteous men were not to be found in Sodom and the town was destroyed, whereas the spiritual dedication and purity of purpose of the Essenes was strong enough to create the environment necessary for the birth of the Messiah, the savior of mankind. When individuals and groups hold high spiritual ideals and are led by the Spirit of God to work in cooperation to fulfill His plan, miracles are commonplace.

A.T. Pierson, a well-known nineteenth-century American Presbyterian pastor and evangelist stated that "there has never been a spiritual awakening in any country or locality that did not begin in united prayer." Why should we expect a lower bar for the coming of the Messiah to save the people of an entire world than to the coming of the Holy Spirit for revival within a nation? Spiritual awakening follows, not precedes, a strong desire for God's presence in our lives. The day of Pentecost was preceded by prayer and supplication of about one hundred and twenty men and women. It should not be surprising that the choosing of Mary as the mother of the coming Messiah, and his subsequent birth, was preceded by the prayers, meditations, dedication, and faithfulness of a community of individuals who dedicated their lives to that event.

According to Catholic Church tradition, a School of Prophets was established by the prophet Elijah at Mount Carmel about twenty miles west of Nazareth near the Mediterranean Sea coast. The Catholic Carmelite Religious Order traces its origin to this School of Prophets and claims that its founders were the prophet Elias [Heb. Elijah] and his immediate successor Eliseus [Heb. Elisha] who lived on Mount Carmel. The order is more properly called the Friars of Blessed Mary of Mount Carmel and therefore recognizes a close connection between Mary, the mother of Jesus, and Mount Carmel, the center of the Essene community.

The readings indicate that the purpose and foundational principles of the Essenes were derived from tenets that had their origins in the teachings of Melchizedek that were studied and propagated by later prophets including Samuel, Elijah, and Elisha [5749-8]. Elijah was instrumental in actually establishing the School of Prophets at Mount Carmel. Mount Carmel is also the place where Elijah defeated and slew the four hundred and fifty prophets of Baal and the four hundred prophets of Asherah after demonstrating that God could produce a burnt offering on an altar saturated with water (1 Kings 18:19–38). In the context of those events, it would seem to be an appropriate place to prepare for the entry of a Messiah who would restore the true relationship between God and man and would bring the hope of salvation to a sin-sick world.

The lives and minds of the founders of the prophetic school and their followers through the centuries were dedicated to bringing about the foretold coming of the Messiah. These men and women incarnated with a single purpose and remained true to that purpose despite the temptations of the material world and the long period of time between the anticipated event and the birth of Jesus. The members of the school sustained their beliefs through their faith and dedication to God and willingness to sacrifice their lives to a greater cause [254-109 and 1472-3].

A remnant of the original School of Prophets survived through the centuries and maintained its purpose and traditions. By the decades before the birth of Jesus the school had evolved into the distinct Jewish religious group called Essenes. By the time of the birth of Jesus, Mount Carmel was home to a major Essene community and the location of a temple that was the spiritual focal point of the group. The readings translated the word Essene as "Expectancy" and stated that the members of the group were anticipating and actively preparing for the birth of the Messiah (Isaiah 53:5). A major aspect of this preparation involved the search for and training of potential mothers who would bear and raise the Messiah.

The writings of first-century historians Philo Judaeus (born 25 BC) and Titus Flavius Josephus (born Joseph ben Matityahu 37 AD) confirm the Essenes as one of three major Jewish religious groups of that period, the other two being the Pharisees and Sadducees. These historians state that the sect arose about 150 BC and disappeared toward the end of the first century A.D. They appeared to have been disbanded or scattered with the Roman invasion of Jerusalem in 70 AD after fulfilling their group purpose to provide the spiritual and physical environment for the long-awaited Messiah.

Their beliefs as described by the historians are as follows: They worshipped one God, Creator and Ruler of all things, and refused to offer blood sacrifices at the Jerusalem Temple, claiming that a reverent mind was the best offering to God. They held that their bodies were corruptible, but were occupied by immortal souls drawn into bodies by some natural longing. All men were regarded as equal and slavery was regarded as contrary to nature. In towns, an officer was appointed to look after travelling brethren. They perpetuated their sect by adopting children and admitting adults chosen as full members after a three-year probationary period.

The Essenes had a monastic community at Qumran, east of Jerusalem, on the western shore of the Dead Sea, and had adherents who lived among the larger Jewish community. The Qumran monastic community would come to prominence nearly two thousand years later as the compilers of the Dead Sea Scrolls found hidden in caves in the cliffs above the community. The existence of the Essenes was implied or mentioned in dozens of readings from about eleven years before the discovery of the scrolls in 1947.

QUESTIONS TO PONDER

1. The Bible is replete with symbolism. What might be the
    symbolic connection between Elijah's defeat of the false
    prophets of Baal and Asherah on Mount Carmel and the
    choice of Mount Carmel as the site of the Essene Temple
    and preparations for the advent of the Messiah?

2. Do you think it is unusual or unlikely that a religious
    school could survive at Mount Carmel for nearly four
    hundred years? What other religious orders survived and
    thrived in the centuries before and after the life of Jesus?
    How long has the Carmelite Religious Order survived?

3. Do you believe that your attitude and behavior toward
    other people influences the future response of other
    people toward you? Do you attract people having similar
    principles and behavioral characteristics to your own
    (like begets like)? If yes, do you think this is a spiritual
    law or simply human nature?

4. Do you believe that a group of cooperative people united
    in prayer and dedication to a spiritual cause can set
    events in motion that can change the world? Can you
    think of any groups in recent history that might qualify?

5. The Bible doesn't mention the Essenes. Of course, the
    Old Testament preceded the existence of the Essenes.
    Why do you think this Jewish sect is not mentioned
    in the New Testament even though they were the

community which provided a spiritually and physically safe environment for Jesus during his infancy and early life? Who was the New Testament written for, who was it written by, and when was it written? When Jesus told people about Himself was He more concerned about describing His birthplace, education, and occupation like so many of us today, or was He more concerned about describing his relationship with God, His role as Messiah, and the need for men everywhere to repent for their sins and change their behavior?

3
THE ESSENE LEADER

(Q) Why was Judy not a boy as expected?

(A) That is from the powers on high, and gave the first demonstration of woman's place in the affairs and associations of man. For, as were the teachings of Jesus, that released woman from that bondage to which she had been held since the ideas of man conceived from the fall of Eve, or of her first acceptance of the opinions, - these were the first, and those activities that brought about, in the teachings materially, that as Jesus proclaimed.

[Edgar Cayce Reading 2067-11]

(Q) Where did Judy receive her education, in what subjects, and who were her teachers?

(A) The Holy Spirit, and the mother and father; not from other sources, though there were those activities from all of the teachings of the East, through those early periods before there were those acceptances of Judy as the leader of the Essenes at Carmel at that period.

[Edgar Cayce Reading 2067-11]

For God is not a God of disorder but of peace. As in all
the congregations of the saints, women should remain
silent in the churches. They are not allowed to speak,
but must be in submission, as the Law says.

(1 Corinthians 14:33-34 NIV)

The Essene community at Mount Carmel was led by a woman named Judy during the period immediately preceding and after the birth of Jesus. She also was the primary spiritual teacher of the young Jesus. Her extensive knowledge of prophesies, traditions, and spiritual visitations within the Jewish and other religious communities was taught to the young Jesus over a period of about five years. The fact that an Essene religious leader was a woman was an unusual occurrence at that time and place in that society, and the appointment of Judy to the leadership position was questioned by some Essene members.

The readings state that this gender choice was divinely inspired, intentional, and part of God's plan. The Apostle Paul, who was raised in a Pharisee family (Acts 23:6), and educated in Jewish Law under the tutelage of the famous Pharisee teacher Gamaliel (Acts 22:3) apparently could not reject his formal training and accept that women could be in a position of religious authority, even when a woman was the primary teacher of moral values, religion, and philosophy to the young Jesus. In his defense, Paul may not have been fully aware of the role of Judy in the Essene community and early education of Jesus.

The readings describe the birth of Judy to Phinehas and Elkatama in about 20 BC as having many common elements to the birth of the prophet Samuel to Elkhanah and Hannah a thousand years earlier (1 Samuel 1:11–20). In the case of both Samuel and Judy, conception followed the aging parent's strong desire for a child and their promise to give the child to God. Both of these promises were fulfilled by dedicating the child to the priest of the temple. In Judy's case, this meant dedication to the Essene Temple at Mount Carmel, not the main Jewish temple in Jerusalem. That the child of Phinehas and Elkatama was born female was unexpected and a source of consternation to her parents, because a son was expected.

The fact that the future leader of the Essenes at Mount Carmel was a woman was part of God's plan to elevate the role of women in the affairs of society and in their relationship and associations with man. Women in the Jewish society at the time of Jesus held a subservient role to men. The status of a women was often considered to be little more than that of chattel or property.

This lowly position was not as God desired, and the authoritative and respected position of Judy as leader of a major religious group through which the Messiah was to be born, would begin the process of returning women to their rightful place as contributors to and leaders in society [2067-11]. The Essene community under the guidance of Judy would not only provide the proper environment for the birth and rearing of the savior of humankind, but would provide an example of the proper role of women in society.

Judy was a prophetess in her own right. She was not formally educated but was home-schooled by her parents during her early years and was self-educated in the years that followed, all guided by the Holy Spirit. Her studies were international in scope and spiritual in nature. In accordance with her future role as the Essene leader, Judy compiled and recorded Jewish traditions relating to the foretold coming of the Messiah. She also collected and compiled Egyptian, Indian, and Persian religious teachings, traditions and philosophies. She studied the experiences of individuals who had received visitations from divine sources in the form of visions and dreams, and organized, recorded and preserved unwritten oral traditions and written records of such events.

Much of this study preceded her appointment and acceptance as leader of the Essenes. By the time of the birth of Jesus or soon thereafter, she had risen to the position of leader of the Essene community at Mount Carmel, and her authority in that position was ultimately acknowledged and respected by the twelve apostles and the Holy Women who aided Jesus during His travels and teaching [1151-10].

QUESTIONS TO PONDER

1. What do you think of a Jewish religious community headed by a woman in that time? Would you consider that to be a radical event that "demonstrate women's place in the affairs of man?" [2067-11]

2. Why would this important Jewish religious group compile records from non-Jewish religious and philosophical

systems? Would we benefit from learning more about
these religions? What standard would we use to discern
truths imbedded in other belief systems? [3344-2]

3. The records of non-Jewish religious teachings that Judy
    compiled were undoubtedly used as teaching material
    in lessons she prepared and presented to Jesus. Also,
    the readings state that Jesus Himself traveled to Persia,
    India, and Egypt for several years to further his educa-
    tion in religion, philosophy, and the strength and protec-
    tion of mental and bodily health. Many Christians today
    not only discount the value of these ancient religions
    and their spiritual texts and traditions, but all too often
    are quick to declare that those who follow these religions
    cannot truly understand God and will not "go to heaven"
    when they die. Does the knowledge that Jesus studied
    these religions in preparation for his ministry change
    your attitude toward persons born into other religious
    traditions? [2067-1]

4. Contrast the status and position of Judy within the
    Essene religious community with the cultural belief
    expressed by Paul in 1 Corinthians 14:34 that women
    should remain silent in religious meetings and matters.
    Although Paul may have had little contact with the
    Essene religious authorities, it is unlikely that he was
    unaware of Judy's role as leader of the Essene religious
    community and primary teacher of the young Jesus
    because she was actively involved with at least some

of the apostles. Was he aware of her role as a religious prophet, leader and teacher, but could not cast aside years of orthodox Jewish religious training to accept her authority and accept women as valued religious leaders? Think about what it took for him to change his mind so that he was able to accept Jesus and His followers?

4
THE FORERUNNER

Behold, I will send you Elijah the prophet before the coming of the great and dreadful day of the LORD.

(Malachi 4:5 KJV)

And thou, child, shalt be called the prophet of the Highest: for thou shalt go before the face of the Lord to prepare his ways.

(Luke 1:76 KJV)

And they asked him, saying, Why say the scribes that Elias must first come? And he answered and told them, Elias verily cometh first, and restoreth all things; and how it is written of the Son of man, that he must suffer many things, and be set at nought. But I say unto you, That Elias is indeed come, and they have done unto him whatsoever they listed, as it is written of him.

(Mark 9:11-13 KJV)

As they were coming down the mountain, Jesus instructed them, "Don't tell anyone what you have seen, until the Son of Man has been raised from the dead." The disciples asked him, "Why then do the teachers of the law say that Elijah must come first?" Jesus replied, "To be sure, Elijah comes and will restore all things.

> *But I tell you, Elijah has already come, and they did*
> *not recognize him, but have done to him everything*
> *they wished. In the same way the Son of Man is going*
> *to suffer at their hands." Then the disciples understood*
> *that he was talking to them about John the Baptist.*
>
> (*Matthew 17:9-13 NIV*)

When the priests and Levites were sent to question John the Baptist about his identity, they asked him if he was the Messiah and if he was Elijah (John 1:21). John answered no to both questions, but instead, emphasized his role as forerunner in laying the foundation, or "making the way straight", for the coming of the Lord. He either was not consciously aware of his previous incarnation as Elijah, or chose to focus the attention of his interrogators on his current activity and purpose instead of his previous incarnation.

Later, when the disciples had seen the transfigured Jesus speaking to Moses and Elijah, they asked Jesus why the scribes (scholars versed in the Mosaic Law) said that Elijah must come again before the Messiah (Malachi 4:5). Jesus tells them that Elijah had already come and that the authorities had done what they wished to him (Mark 9:11), referring to the beheading of John the Baptist by Herod Antipas, tetrarch of Galilee.

The Pharisee priests, Levites, Jewish scribes, and Jesus himself saw nothing unusual in the question or the concept that a soul could incarnate as both Elijah and John the Baptist. As Elijah, this soul established the School of Prophets that would prepare for, and keep alive the thought and anticipation of, the foretold Messiah for four hundred years. The School of Prophets survived and evolved into the Essene community that protected and nurtured the young Jesus. As John the Baptist, the same soul announced to the world beyond the Essene community that the Messiah had arrived and made the final preparation for the ministry of Jesus. His efforts and role as forerunner spanned centuries, not just a few years.

The parents of John were Zacharias (Heb. Zachariah) and Elizabeth. Zacharias was a member of the orthodox priesthood with responsibilities at the Jewish temple and access to the Holy of Holies of the Inner Court. It is not certain if Zacharias was a Pharisee or Sadducee; the more important point is that Elizabeth was a member of the Essene community. This fact was not entirely acceptable to his fellow priests, and it caused Zacharias to keep his wife in their residence in the countryside [5749-8].

It was not unusual or a burden for a priest to live outside of Jerusalem because they were not required to be at the temple every day. Zacharias was a priest of the division of Abijah (Luke 1:5), one of twenty-four priestly divisions responsible for serving in the temple at Jerusalem (1 Chronicles 24:7–18). These divisions performed their temple service in rotation, each period of service lasting one week, and the priests stayed at their own residences between periods of service.

When Zacharias was offering incense at the altar, he was visited by the angel Gabriel who announced to the fearful priest that his prayers were to be answered and that his wife Elizabeth was to bear a son, who was to be called John. This son would walk in the spirit and power of Elias and would prepare the hearts of a disobedient people for the Lord (Luke 1:13–16). When Zacharias disputed with Gabriel as to whether such an event could happen because of his and Elizabeth's advanced age, he was made to lose his voice until the birth of his son. This prevented Zacharias from giving the blessing to the awaiting people at the end of his service and from announcing the angel's visit.

By the time of the birth of John, Zacharias had come to believe in the Essene prophesy of the imminent coming of the Messiah and believe that his son would have a role in the event. The fact that he openly declared this belief to fellow priests within his division made him a pariah and heretic in their eyes, and they murdered him "with his hands upon the horns of the altar" as he performed his priestly duties [5749-8]. Zacharias becomes the first recorded martyr for what will become Christianity. The murder brought fear among the Essenes for the safety of the Messiah and was the catalyst that caused the group to advance preparations for the wedding of Joseph and Mary and birth of the Christ child, and also to make preparations for the child's protection.

Jesus later chastises the scribes and Pharisees for their long history of failure to recognize prophets sent by God and their murder of many of them from the days of Abel to the recent death of Zacharias (Mat 23:35 and Luke 11:51). He explicitly mentions that the death of Zacharias occurred between the temple (or sanctuary) and the altar but does not identify him as the father of John the Baptist.

Modern scholars state that Jesus was referring to the murder of the Old Testament prophet Zachariah who died about 550

B.C. For what reason would Jesus tell the Pharisees of his day that they were responsible for murders that took place from the time of Abel to a time one-half a millennium before they were born? Instead, the accusation was a direct reference to the blood on their hands because of the murder of the father of John the Baptist, as well as a general indictment of the religious authorities for being more concerned with protecting their power, perceived religious authority and the law of their ancestors rather than being perceptive and attentive to God's prophets and receptive of their messages to mankind.

QUESTIONS TO PONDER

1. The common interpretation of the words of Jesus concerning the nature of John the Baptist by biblical scholars and laypersons is that John had the same qualities or temperament (spirit) of Elijah. Yet, the prophet Malachi stated that God would send Elijah the prophet to prepare the way for the Lord (Mal 4:5) and Jesus clearly stated that John was Elijah who was to come (Mat 11:13–15; Mat 17:10–13; Mar 9:11–13). Why do Christian theologians so adamantly refuse to accept a literal interpretation of these verses and fail to take them at face value, yet choose to interpret many symbolic and obscure verses in the Old Testament and Revelation as literal facts?

2. John the Baptist stated that he was not Elijah when asked by the priests and Levites (John 1:21)? Why did

he contradict Jesus? Note that research into past life claims almost completely focus on statements made by children between the ages of two and seven because past-life memories are lost as children grow older (see, for example, published research and research summaries by Ian Stevenson, former Carlson professor of psychiatry and director of the division of personality studies at the University of Virginia). If John had acknowledged that he was Elijah reincarnated, would this announcement have interfered with his mission as forerunner for Jesus?

3. Was the beheading of John the Baptist at the beginning of the ministry of Jesus necessary to transfer the attention of his followers and new spiritual seekers from him toward Jesus? That is, was John the Baptist sacrificed as part of God's plan to advance the mission of Jesus? Or was it simply one of many political murders of that day? What deeds performed by Elijah might indicate that John was reaping the fruits of his previous actions as the prophet?

4. In their arrogance and belief that the Jewish scriptures were the final word from God and the full truth of His relationship with man, the religious authorities were closed-minded to the fact that God was not finished revealing new truths to mankind; at least, not if those revelations failed to coincide with their preconceived ideas. Are religious authorities today equally closed-minded to the possibility that God is not finished

revealing Himself to man? How should a claim of new revelation be tested to distinguish between God's Truth and man's arrogance and delusion that he already knows it all?

5
THE MOTHER

(Q) Was Ann prepared for her part in the drama as mother of Mary?

(A) Only as in the general, not as specific as Mary after Mary being pointed out. See, there was no belief in the fact that Ann proclaimed that the child was without father. It's like many proclaiming today that the Master was immaculately conceived; they say "Impossible!" They say that it isn't in compliance with the natural law. It IS a natural law, as has been indicated by the projection of mind into matter and thus making of itself a separation to become encased in same … [In] this particular period with Ann and then the Master AS the son; but the ONLY begotten of the Father in the flesh AS a son OF an immaculately conceived daughter!

[Edgar Cayce Reading 5749-8]

Much might be given as to how or why and when there were the purposes that brought about the materialization of Jesus in the flesh. In giving then the history: There were those in the faith of the fathers to whom the promises were given that these would be fulfilled as from the beginning of man's record. Hence there was the continued preparation and dedication of those who might be the channels through which this chosen vessel might enter - through choice - into materiality.

Thus in Carmel - where there were the priests of this faith - there were the maidens chosen that were dedicated to this purpose, this office, this service. Among them was Mary, the beloved, the chosen one; and she, as had been foretold, was chosen as the channel. Thus she was separated and kept in the closer associations with and in the care or charge of this office. That was the beginning, that was the foundation of what ye term the Church.

[Edgar Cayce Reading 5749-7]

It was the practice of the Essene community at Mount Carmel to accept young girls for training as potential mothers of the Messiah. Parents chose to dedicate their children to the community for that purpose, and the community accepted only those children who they deemed to be perfect in body and in mind.

Ann, the mother of Mary, dedicated her child to the Essene Temple for service and training when she was about three years of age. There was some confusion and resistance in the community as to whether this child should be accepted, because Ann claimed that she had conceived Mary without knowing a man. Some in the community questioned the veracity of the statement, and disagreements among the members led to a difference of opinion about the wisdom of accepting Mary.

Despite the controversy, Mary was eventually accepted because she was declared perfect in body and mind by those who examined her. Although many girls were presented to the community for temple service, only twelve girls were selected to receive the special training required for potential mothers of the Messiah [5749-8]. Mary became one of the chosen twelve.

The readings that describe the dedication of Mary are supported by Catholic tradition and by similar descriptions of her dedication in two apocryphal gospels, the Protoevangel of James and the Gospel of the Nativity of Mary. These documents name the parents of Mary as Joachim and Anna; Joachim being a descendant of the royal family of David and Anna being a descendant of the priestly family of Aaron. Thus, the lineage of Mary and Jesus included both royal and priestly Jewish families.

Mary's aged parents are said to have asked God for a child and made a vow before her birth to dedicate her to the Lord. By Catholic tradition, the child was conceived by God. At age three, she was presented at the temple, where she mounted the stairs alone and made a vow of virginity. She remained in the temple where she was educated with other Jewish children who had been presented to the temple, and she is said to have experienced ecstatic visions and visits from angels during her life there. This tradition was strong enough to cause the early Catholic Church to establish and celebrate a Feast of the Presentation of the Blessed Virgin Mary.

The readings state that each child completed a rigorous training program for physical and mental strength as part of the preparation for motherhood. Mary's training and education lasted more than a decade after her dedication to the Essene community, all designed to prepare her for the long-anticipated moment when the Messiah would be born. A regime of physical exercises ensured that the young bodies developed normally and built strength and stamina. Meals were planned and prepared in ways that kept the food nourishing and the body healthy. The training instilled them with the bodily strength and knowledge necessary to provide the child proper physical nourishment. Mental exercises were also part of the training, and included the concepts of chastity and purity to shield the young girls from worldly temptations that could endanger the success of the Messiah's birth and rearing. The mental training helped the girls develop the mental focus and stamina that would keep them grounded in the spiritual foundation of the holy mission.

Love and patience were taught, being qualities that would make a loving mother strong in faith and single-minded in purpose. Endurance was taught so that the mother might stand strong when faced with life situations that could threaten the young Messiah or the family that protected Him. Specific details of the training are not given in the readings, but they are described as being severe and possibly would be considered persecutions in today's society. Mary was chosen to be the mother of the Messiah because out of the twelve maidens in training at the Essene Temple, she was the person who most demonstrated the moral qualities and mental attitude essential for the mother of the Messiah. She was well-prepared to give Jesus a loving home environment that would let him grow physically, emotionally, and spiritually into a healthy young man until He was able to become consciously aware of His higher purpose and ready to accept and fulfill His role as the channel through which God would work His will for mankind.

The choice of Mary as the future mother of the Christ child was not made during a private angelic vision that could only be seen within the mind of Mary, but was a public visitation by the angel Gabriel that was seen and accepted by the group of Essene priests and members responsible for raising and teaching the girls. The twelve girls were selected by the Essene priests for their potential because they were thought to have the special spiritual, mental, and physical qualities appropriate to the mother of the Messiah, but God through His angel made the final decision as to which girl would be the chosen one. Mary was between twelve and thirteen years of age when she was chosen to be the mother of the Messiah and had spent ten years in training at Mount Carmel. She spent another three to four years in additional training before she became pregnant with Jesus and was married to Joseph.

The choice of Mary from among the twelve candidates was made at the Mount Carmel Temple on the steps that led to an altar where the twelve candidates gathered early in the morning. The lead individual in the procession up the stairs to the altar varied from morning to morning. On this particular and special day, Mary led the group of candidates, and when she reached the top step there was a flash of lightening and a clap of thunder. The angel Gabriel took the hand of Mary and led her before the altar, thus indicating to the priests in attendance that she was the one chosen by God to become the mother of the coming Messiah. The morning sun bathed the young girls as they made their way up the steps to the altar for prayer and the burning of incense, which marked the beginning of their daily training ritual. The readings describe the event as a beautiful scene with all clothed in the morning rays "as in purple and gold" in reference to the physical and spiritual majesty of the moment [5749-8].

QUESTIONS TO PONDER

1. Is the concept that Mary was conceived in Anna's womb by the action of Spirit instead of man any more difficult for you to believe than the widely accepted idea in Christianity that Jesus was conceived in Mary's womb by the action of Spirit instead of man?

2. The readings state that Mary was trained for more than twelve years by individuals dedicating their lives to the coming of the Messiah. Does the explanation that Mary was trained for her role as mother of Jesus, with the ability to make choices regarding her acceptance of that role, make her story more or less plausible than the traditional concept of an unprepared village girl being told by an angel that she will be the mother of the Messiah?

3. There are several instances in the Old Testament when elder couples ask God for a child and promise to dedicate that child to God. Does the soul that subsequently

incarnates in the newborn infant's body have prior
knowledge of that promise? Has that soul already made
a free-will decision to make every effort to honor and be
a part of that promise? If yes, how might the attractions
of a physical body immersed in a sensory and sensual
material existence derail the spiritual mission of the soul
before the child attains an age where it can become physically conscious of that promise?.

4. What would be your reaction if your daughter stated
   she was pregnant, and then claimed the father was God?
   How might your reaction be different if you were a
   member of a religious community that expected such
   an event and was dedicated to living righteous lives to
   facilitate the unfolding of the event? As an outsider,
   would we be more likely to consider such a community
   to be a freak cult or accept their claims without question? What do you think was the generally accepted view
   of mainstream Jews about the Essene community and its
   proclaimed mission?

6

THE EARTHLY FATHER

This is how the birth of Jesus Christ came about: His mother Mary was pledged to be married to Joseph, but before they came together, she was found to be with child through the Holy Spirit. Because Joseph her husband was a righteous man and did not want to expose her to public disgrace, he had in mind to divorce her quietly. But after he had considered this, an angel of the Lord appeared to him in a dream and said, "Joseph son of David, do not be afraid to take Mary home as your wife, because what is conceived in her is from the Holy Spirit. She will give birth to a son, and you are to give him the name Jesus, because he will save his people from their sins." All this took place to fulfill what the Lord had said through the prophet: "The virgin will be with child and will give birth to a son, and they will call him Immanuel" -- which means, "God with us." When Joseph woke up, he did what the angel of the Lord had commanded him and took Mary home as his wife.

(Matthew 1:18-24 NIV)

Mary and Joseph were chosen by God to be the channels through which the child Jesus would be born and raised, thereby fulfilling the Old Testament prophecies concerning the coming of a Messiah that would save His people. Marriages between children of Jewish families were usually arranged by the parents in the age when the Essenes were preparing for the Messiah's birth. The parents of the future couple usually drew up a contract to seal the agreement. These contracts were often made years before the children were legally old enough to marry. Counter to this tradition, the families of Mary and Joseph did not enter into a contractual arrangement on their behalf. The choice of a spouse for Mary was the responsibility of the leaders of the Essene community, but this choice was directed by divine influence within the leadership and by consensual agreement between Mary and Joseph [5749-8].

Joseph was chosen by the sect to be Mary's spouse soon after her selection as mother of the Messiah by the angel Gabriel. Joseph did not claim his bride until three or four years later when she had completed her training at Mount Carmel. He was chosen from among the Essene men who had separated and dedicated themselves in body, in mind, in spirit specifically for this coming of the Messiah. An important factor in this choice was his perceived spiritual kinship with Mary. He was not chosen because of age or because of his lineal descent from the house of David [5749-7]. Mary and Joseph probably were acquainted with each other because of their activities in the Essene community, but they did not meet or socialize with each other before their wedding day.

Joseph was thirty-six years old and Mary was sixteen years old when they were married. Mary was found to be pregnant at the completion of her training and before her marriage. Joseph became concerned and skeptical about his chosen role because of what others would say about the large age difference between the couple and about her pregnant condition. These concerns were tempered by the assurance from the Essene brethren as to the divine nature of the choice and were completely removed by the guidance and support he received through dreams and the visitation from the angel Gabriel, who reassured Joseph and told him that the child is of God and is to be named Jesus [5749-8].

The wedding ceremony followed the customs of traditional Jewish weddings. However, it was more than a ceremony. It was also the recognition of the spiritual purpose of the union and celebration of hope for the future represented in the Messiah. The marriage did not replace or override the wishes of the couple but strengthened the desires and purposes within their hearts and the Essene community [254-109].

During the first year of marriage, Joseph lived in Nazareth where he operated a carpentry business and Mary divided her time between living in the Judean countryside (perhaps near Elizabeth who was preparing to give birth to John who became the Baptist) and staying with Joseph. They were living in Nazareth when the Roman decree went out for the Jews to travel to the city of their ancestry to be registered for taxation.

The couple remained celibate for the first ten years of their marriage, dedicating their lives to the care of their child Jesus, who spent much time being educated by the Essene leader Judy and others in the Essene community who held joint responsibility for his rearing and education. About ten years after their marriage, they began the normal life of a married couple and had children of their own.

QUESTION TO PONDER

1. Being the earthly father of Jesus did not entitle Joseph to a monthly stipend from God for the care and feeding of the young Jesus. Joseph worked as a carpenter to provide an income with which to support his family, and likely also shared in the material resources of the Essene community which held produced and earned goods in common. What does this say about our expectations for God to provide for us? Are we required to act as well as ask?

2. When Lazarus became sick, his sisters Mary and Martha sent word to Jesus of his sickness in the hope that he would be healed. Jesus intentionally delayed seeing Lazarus until it was too late and he had died, for the express purpose of glorifying God and demonstrating His position as the Son of God (John 11:1–45). The readings state that Jesus was called back from Persia, where He was studying, because of the death of His earthly father Joseph [5749-7]. Why did He not take this opportunity to restore the life of Joseph as He later did for His friend Lazarus [5749-16]? (Note that the death of Joseph occurred well before Jesus completed His spiritual

training and initiation in Egypt, and before He began
His active ministry).

3. Joseph had serious concerns about his role as the earthly
    father of the Messiah after learning that Mary was
    already pregnant before their wedding. God allayed his
    fears by sending an angel to give him a message through
    the medium of a dream. The same method was used
    after the death of Herod to inform Joseph that it was safe
    for his family to leave Egypt and return home. The Old
    Testament is filled with similar stories where God uses
    dreams to communicate with the Israelites and their
    neighbors. Dreams arise at the soul level and are a pow-
    erful medium for communication between the spiritual
    world and the physical world [5754-3]. Have you ever
    had a dream that imparted warning, encouragement,
    advice, or even precognition? Are informative dreams
    more likely to be remembered by the conscious mind
    of individuals who make an active attempt to receive
    and catalog them? The physical mind can be trained to
    remember and be more receptive to the nightly dreams
    that originate in the subconscious mind. Do you believe
    the study of dreams can yield valuable spiritual insights
    and help guide the spiritual progress of an individual?

7

THE IMMACULATE CONCEPTION

Because Joseph her husband was a righteous man and did not want to expose her to public disgrace, he had in mind to divorce her quietly. But after he had considered this, an angel of the Lord appeared to him in a dream and said, "Joseph son of David, do not be afraid to take Mary home as your wife, because what is conceived in her is from the Holy Spirit."

(Matthew 1:19-20 NIV)

(Q) Explain the immaculate conception.

(A) As [Living] flesh is the activity of the mental being (or the spiritual self and mental being, the soul) pushing itself into matter. Spirit - as He gave - is neither male nor female, they are then both - or one. And when man had reached that period of the full separation from Creative Forces in the spirit, then flesh as man knows it today became in material plane a reality. Then, the immaculate conception is the physical and mental so attuned to spirit as to be quickened [to spring to life; to become animated] by same. Hence the spirit, the soul, of the Master then was brought into being [incarnated into the material

world] through the accord of the Mother in materiality, that ye know in the earth as conception.

[Edgar Cayce Reading 5749-7]

Souls enter the material world every day [3744-5]. This is
a natural law that connects the conscious spiritual awareness of
a soul mind with the biological development and physical birth
of a human body. Although conception marks the beginning of
cell division and the growth of a fetus in the womb, the soul typ-
ically does not take full control of the infant body until immediately before or shortly after it is born [457-10]. This is reasonable
because otherwise two souls could compete for mastery of the
body of the mother. The physical and biological laws known to
modern science do not as yet include or recognize a relation
between spirit, mind, and the material universe of atomic matter
and energy. Scientists have not yet identified souls as the source
of bodily animation in individuals.

There is strong circumstantial evidence from reincarnation
research conducted by Ian Stevenson at the University of Virginia
School of Medicine that souls choose the newborn infant they
will inhabit and may monitor the progress of a fetus and events
occurring in the lives of its parents before the birth. The readings mention a soul that rejected an opportunity to incarnate,
causing the infant body to be born dead (stillborn), because the
future father broke a promise made to the incarnating soul in the
spiritual realm [2390-2]. Apparently, the potential father broke
his promise by drinking alcohol heavily during his life and the

incoming soul refused to become trapped in that type of environment. Presumably, the promise was extracted because of a previous undesirable life situation involving alcohol abuse.

Human flesh is animated only if a soul (a composite unit of spirit and mind controlled by will) pushes itself into the physical world and links with the body of the newborn infant. This amazing union or interface of spirit and mind with the flesh of a material body occurs with every live birth. Both the Bible (Genesis 2:7) and the readings [5749-7] refer to this activity as creating living flesh or a living soul, indicating that biological human flesh is not truly alive until it has been quickened by the activity of spirit or soul.

The spiritual and mental desires of the parents during conception and gestation as well as the desire, purpose, and spiritual requirements of the incarnating soul determine which soul will be attracted to the new body [281-53] and become the primary spiritual influence in the life of the young child [281-54]. Mary, or any of the other young female candidates dedicated to the Essene community, could only become the mother of Jesus if the act of conception was accomplished by her full physical and spiritual consent and her complete mental attunement to the purposes of God concerning the coming of the Messiah.

The action that caused Mary to conceive is described as a quickening of the womb of Mary by the direct action of the Mind and Spirit of God and the soul of Jesus on the reproductive organs in the physical body of Mary. This conception was not perpetrated by God upon the unsuspecting person of Mary without her prior knowledge or consent. The action required that Mary's body be physically healthy with all organs working in harmony and that her mental desire and will be focused toward and dedicated to the spiritual purpose embodied in the incarnation of the Messiah [2072-3]. Mary was a willing and necessary participant in this act of spiritual conception. Mary's body had to be purified and sanctified and her mind attuned and consecrated to that high and holy purpose before conception could occur.

Note that the concept of Immaculate Conception as taught by the Catholic Church does not refer to Mary conceiving Jesus without having had sexual relations with a man, but is an expression of the idea that Mary herself was born in a sinless state by the grace of God so that she would be prepared to bear the Messiah. The meaning of immaculate conception as described in the readings refers to conception in the absence of a human father [5749-7]. The readings do also state that Mary was conceived without the need for an earthly father which suggests that she, like Jesus, was also born as a perfected soul and was fully committed to her future role of bringing the Messiah into the world.

The human conscious mind finds it difficult to comprehend that Mary could have conceived without sexual intercourse and this difficulty can become a stumbling block to the understanding and acceptance of Jesus as a historical figure and Messiah. Scientific medical studies cannot confirm this possibility because its investigative techniques are confined to the realm of atomic matter and energy and do not acknowledge or detect spirit. However, the Bible and the readings indicate that souls can and have entered the earth through a variety of means that did not involve sexual intercourse. In the case of both Anna and her

DNA?

daughter Mary, conception and the subsequent birth of a physical body occurred because of the action of spirit on female reproductive organs, but only after the bodies of the future mothers were purified and made holy in purpose.

The body of Adam was intentionally designed and created for the habitation of a soul using the same elements that comprise the earth, but was originally more thought form than solid matter. This new creature was activated by the breath of God, meaning the action of spirit and soul incarnation. The physical body of Adam would have been no more than an inanimate biological shell if it had not been occupied by a soul and became a living being (Gen 2:7). The readings state that the entry of Melchizedek into the earth was facilitated through activity born of his desire to form a quasi-physical body by direct manipulation of matter by spirit [2072-4], an act which is reminiscent of the resurrection of Jesus. The Bible confirms this otherworldly aspect of Melchizedek's appearance in the earth (Heb 7:3).

By fulfilling God's commandment to Adam to overcome the earth, Jesus became one with and master of the laws of the universe. The soul of Jesus was able to create a new thought-form body after it was separated from His old physical body by death on the cross. The New Testament calls this action resurrection of the body. This new insubstantial body was similar in nature to the original body of Adam and the body of Melchizedek. The immaculate conception of Jesus by Mary seems miraculous and beyond the realm of possibility to our physical consciousness, but is well within the system of laws that define the interface between the spiritual and material worlds.

QUESTION TO PONDER

1. Reading 544-1 states, "For, in the earth the body is the
    temple of the living soul. And here in the temple may
    one meet with one's Maker and thus become aware of
    His consciousness dwelling within, and of self being
    - through the knowledge of self, physically and men-
    tally - in accord with those purposes for the fulfilling
    of those activities He would bring in the experience."
    How was Jesus able to remain single-mindedly focused
    on His spiritual purpose throughout His entire life even
    unto death on the cross? Was it possible for Him to lose
    sight of his spiritual purpose because of the allure of the
    physical world?

2. The readings state that souls are neither male nor female
    but that souls have an active positive aspect and a passive
    negative aspect (this means polarity, not good versus
    bad). Jesus touched on this subject when He said there
    is no marriage in heaven (Mat 22:30). One or the other
    of these attributes normally dominates according to the
    sexuality of the body that the soul occupies [5749-7]. Do
    you think male and female humans normally express
    active and passive traits, respectively?

3. In the Gospel According to Thomas, a quasi-Gnostic
    writing, Jesus is quoted as saying "When you make the
    two one, … the male and the female one and the same,
    so that the male not be male nor the female; …; then

will you enter the kingdom." What might be the spiritual meaning and purpose of making the male and female as one?

4. Do you think Jesus made the male and female as one in his personality? What personality traits and actions might make you think yes or no? What qualities and attributes did He display that we might think of as more masculine or more feminine?

8
THE INN AND THE BIRTH

Therefore the Lord himself will give you a sign: The virgin will be with child and will give birth to a son, and will call him Immanuel.

(Isaiah 7:14 NIV)

So Joseph also went up from the town of Nazareth in Galilee to Judea, to Bethlehem the town of David, because he belonged to the house and line of David. He went there to register with Mary, who was pledged to be married to him and was expecting a child. While they were there, the time came for the baby to be born, and she gave birth to her firstborn, a son. She wrapped him in cloths and placed him in a manger, because there was no room for them in the inn.

(Luke 2:4-7 NIV)

While among the entity's stables was indeed the place of rest, it was because of the very rabble, the very act of those that were in authority - both as to the Roman as well as the various groups that were in their discussions making for the very things that would hinder or prevent those experiences that had been foretold. The entity did this rather for protection, than because - as has been said - there was "no room in the Inn." But this was meant to be implied or conveyed, that they were "turned away." Yet in the entity's activities it was really for the protection. For the entity, too, had seen a vision; the entity, too, had heard, had known of the voices that were in the air. The entity, too, had seen the star in the east. The entity, too, had known of those experiences that must befall those that were making all the preparations possible under those existent conditions for Him that should come as a teacher, as a shepherd, as a savior.

[Edgar Cayce Reading 1196-2]

The Essene community looked after its members. Historians of the first and second century record procedures for the protection of travelling Essene members. Flavius Josephus stated that many Essenes dwelled in every city, and that an officer was appointed in towns to look after travelling brethren by opening their homes and sharing their possessions with any of their sect who came from other places. Since this was a common practice of the Essene community, it would be certain that Joseph and the pregnant Mary would have been accorded assistance and protection during their trip to Bethlehem and arrangements would have been made for food and shelter.

The readings confirm that Joseph and Mary did not travel alone to Bethlehem and did not wait until they arrived there to randomly search for a promising inn and inquire about a room. Their destination and arrangements for a proper place for overnight stay were prepared in advance, especially considering the possible imminent birth of the Messiah. The safety of the Messiah was never left to chance, but was a priority consideration of the Essene leadership and community. The couple was accompanied by some of Joseph's co-workers and friends, shepherds from Nazareth, and by Josie who Judy had appointed to be a handmaiden and mid-wife to Mary. Because of Mary's physical condition, the progress of the group was slow and it was evening before they arrived at their destination.

The road from Jerusalem to Bethlehem was crowded with many other people traveling between cities and from the countryside to their place of birth, as required by the Roman authorities (Luke 2:1-3) for the census and assessment of their ability to pay taxes [5749-15]. Lodging would have been at a premium. Joseph and Mary with the attendant group responsible for their safe travel arrived at the inn where they planned to spend the night just as the sun was setting. The group was met at the door of the inn by the innkeeper, Apsafar, and the words of the innkeeper, "No room in the Inn" (Luke 2:7), as recorded in the Bible and in the readings are essentially the same, but the meaning and intention are interpreted differently.

Apsafar was a Jewish member of the Essene community and was well aware of the teachings and prophesies of the Essenes about the coming Messiah. He also was aware of the advanced pregnancy of Mary and the potential for the birth to occur soon. The traditional interpretation of his refusal to give them a room is a callous refusal to accommodate Joseph and Mary, causing them to quickly search out a nearby stable for refuge [1196-2]. The actual reason for the words "No room in the Inn," according to the readings, was to get the couple away from the rowdy crowd that filled the inn and away from the eyes of the Roman governing authorities and Jewish religious authorities that frequented the inn [5749-15]. The Essene beliefs and activities leading up to the birth of the Messiah could not have gone entirely unnoticed by the Roman authorities, whose profession or perceived duty was to assess the pulse of the Jewish people and forestall any activity that could become a threat to that authority.

The common interpretation of the biblical account of the encounter between Apsafar and Joseph does not do justice to the efforts of Apsafar to protect the special couple. The sight of the older Joseph and much younger and very pregnant Mary standing at the door of the inn had already caused some of the more crude guests to burst out in jeers and laughter. Even so, the announcement by the innkeeper that no room was available disappointed Joseph and Mary, who were already tired from the long day of travel. The words also caused consternation among their fellow travelers when they realized that Mary had been refused a room.

The readings state that Apsafar had already been forewarned by a vision that the birth could occur during the couple's stay at the inn and that he had already prepared a sheltered and protected place in a nearby cave used as a stable. Mary would find a safe haven in which to rest and have peace and quiet away from the noise and unwanted attention of the crowd inside the inn.

The daughter of the innkeeper, who had already helped clean and prepare the stable, led the couple to the place of shelter.

The birth itself was accompanied by a spectacular supernatural event seen and recognized by many people in the area, but unrecognized or dismissed by many others. Those who looked forward to the coming of a Messiah and those who were receptive to God's influence in the world could sense the pivoting of world history and hear or see nature's response to the birth. Those who had wandered far from their spiritual heritage and were absorbed in self-centeredness and the attractions of material existence sensed nothing unusual, or dismissed the emotions that they felt as an overactive imagination or too much wine. It is the same with us today. We are better able to recognize God at work among us when we are actively seeking him and have attuned ourselves to be receptive to his presence. One reading clearly sums up the undercurrent of mixed emotions among the people near the inn and stable in the minutes leading up to the most important event in world history, the birth of the Messiah.

> Then, - when hope seemed gone, - the herald angels sang. The star appeared, that made the wonderment to the shepherds, that caused the awe and consternation to all of those about the Inn; some making fun, some smitten with conviction that those unkind things said must needs be readjusted in their relationships to things coming to pass. All were in awe as the brightness of His star appeared and shone, as the music of the spheres brought that joyful choir, "Peace on earth! Good will to men of good faith" All

felt the vibrations and saw a great light, - not only the shepherds above that stable but those in the Inn as well. To be sure, those conditions were later to be dispelled by the doubters, who told the people that they had been overcome with wine or what not.

Just as the midnight hour came, there was the birth of the Master.

[Edgar Cayce Reading 5749-15]

QUESTIONS TO PONDER

1. Tradition suggests that Joseph and Mary traveled to Bethlehem alone. Their request for lodging at an inn was rejected and a frantic search for shelter led them to find a nearby stable, now considered a symbol of the humble nature of the coming Messiah. The readings state that Joseph and Mary were accompanied by friends from the Essene community, they were denied a room in the inn for their personal protection, and they were moved to the inn's stable for security and privacy. Which description of events do you think is more plausible?

2. Midnight is the darkest hour of the day. The Bible and the readings frequently use light as a symbol for spiritual illumination from God and darkness as a symbol for the absence of God and presence of sin. Can you think of any spiritual significance to the fact that Jesus was born at midnight?

3. As the anticipated time of the birth of Jesus approached,
    the Essenes were more and more perceived as a threat by
    larger established religious groups such as the Pharisees
    and Sadducees, and by the Romans. Zacharias, the
    husband of Elizabeth, was killed when he expressed
    belief in the Essene teachings about the coming Messiah.
    Herod tried to eliminate a perceived future threat to the
    political order by killing all children under the age of
    two years. Why were such extreme actions precipitated
    by those in authority? Would such unreasonable mea-
    sures to silence a baby have occurred if Mary and Joseph
    were only unassuming inhabitants of the small town of
    Nazareth and not associated with the larger and more
    visible Essene religious organization with its professed
    belief in a coming Messiah?

REFERENCES AND COMMENTS

Chapter 1: Coercion or Calling

1. Jesus relinquished his will and accepted God's will in the Garden of Gethsemane. He knew that decision would lead him to an agonizing death on the cross, but he also knew it was necessary to prepare the way for mankind to eventually reject the material world and return to companionship with God.

   Then Jesus went with his disciples to a place called Gethsemane, and he said to them, "Sit here while I go over there and pray." He took Peter and the two sons of Zebedee along with him, and he began to be sorrowful and troubled. Then he said to them, "My soul is overwhelmed with sorrow to the point of death. Stay here and keep watch with me." Going a little farther, he fell with his face to the ground and prayed, "My Father, if it is possible, may this cup be taken from me. Yet not as I will, but as you will." (Matthew 26:36–39 NIV)

2. Saul (later called Paul) was more than a man who chose to reject Jesus. He was a zealous leader in the active persecution of Christians, those who had chosen to follow the teachings of Jesus. Had Paul simply chosen to not

believe in the teachings of Jesus, he could have remained in that state of mind without God's interference. His desire to destroy the lives of Christians and cripple the nascent Christian church caused God to take direct action against him. He was still given a choice about the direction his future would take, but was no longer permitted to let his choices interfere with the desires of new Christians to follow their own beliefs.

Meanwhile, Saul was still breathing out murderous threats against the Lord's disciples. He went to the high priest and asked him for letters to the synagogues in Damascus, so that if he found any there who belonged to the Way, whether men or women, he might take them as prisoners to Jerusalem. As he neared Damascus on his journey, suddenly a light from heaven flashed around him. He fell to the ground and heard a voice say to him, "Saul, Saul, why do you persecute me?" "Who are you, Lord?" Saul asked. "I am Jesus, whom you are persecuting," he replied. (Acts 9:1–5 NIV)

Chapter 2: The School of Prophets and the Essenes

1.   Edgar Cayce Reading 254-109; 2441-2; 3652-1: The main purpose of the Essene community at Mount Carmel was to train and prepare promising young girls to be the mother of the coming Messiah. It was not their purpose to establish a new religion or to send missionaries throughout the world to spread the message of a coming

Messiah. This message and the need for repentance and a return to God had already been the focus of the Old Testament prophets. The mission of the Essenes was to make ready for the culmination of the prophecies and climactic event of the birth of the Messiah by ensuring that the newborn child had the proper parents and upbringing that would allow the Messiah to accomplish his purpose for the benefit of mankind.

2.   Edgar Cayce Reading 254-109; 5264-1: The Essene community and the purpose that caused the religious community to be formed and kept it together for so many years had its origin in the activities of the Old Testament prophets. Although the community is today considered one of the three major Jewish religious sects, that may be an incorrect perception. The readings state that the Essene community accepted both Jews and Gentiles into their ranks, and perhaps should more appropriately be viewed as an ecumenical organization devoted to the purpose of seeing the prophesy of the Messiah fulfilled than promoting the Jewish religion and Mosaic Laws.

3.   Edgar Cayce Reading 1472-3; 2067-11: By the time Phinehas and Elkatma become associated with and active in the Essene community about twenty four years or more before the birth of Jesus, the original School of Prophets was in a state of decline. The school had been formed four hundred years before and had probably survived many threats to its existence during that long

period, but had almost succumbed to the difficulty of maintaining focus on its mission through changes of leadership and attrition during such a long wait while God's plan unfolded in his own time.

4. Bréhier, E. 1911. Philo Judæus. In The Catholic Encyclopedia. New York, NY: Robert Appleton Company.

5. Hoeber, K. 1910. Flavius Josephus. In The Catholic Encyclopedia. New York, NY: Robert Appleton Company.

6. Graham, E. 1909. Essenes. In The Catholic Encyclopedia. New York, NY: Robert Appleton Company.

7. Kittler, Glenn D, 2018: Edgar Cayce on the Dead Sea Scrolls, A.R.E. Press.

8. Orr, J. Edwin, 1976; The Role of Prayer in Spiritual Awakening, Presented at the National Prayer Congress in Dallas, TX, October 26-29, 1976.

9. Towns, Elmer and Porter, Douglas, 2000: The Ten Greatest Revivals Ever, Destiny Image Publishers.

10. The Essenes were a close knit community that provided their traveling brethren food and shelter and the protection and comfort of a home away from home.

Josephus, Flavius; The Wars Of The Jews, Book II, Chapter 8, paragraph 4: They [the Essenes] have no one certain city, but many of them dwell in every city; and if any of their sect come from other places, what they have lies open for them, just as if it were their own; and they go in to such as they never knew before, as if they had been ever so long acquainted with them. For which reason they carry nothing at all with them when they travel into remote parts, though still they take their weapons with them, for fear of thieves. Accordingly, there is, in every city where they live, one appointed particularly to take care of strangers, and to provide garments and other necessaries for them.

This historical description of traveling Essenes is reminiscent of the biblical verse where Jesus tells his disciples to carry a sword with them when they travel. Perhaps this statement is a reflection of the Essene rule that carrying a sword for protection from thieves is a necessity even for the spiritually minded. It is simply a fact of life in the society of men. Also, Jesus implies that it may be necessary because he will no longer be with them.

Then Jesus asked them, "When I sent you without purse, bag or sandals, did you lack anything?" "Nothing," they answered. He said to them, "But now if you have a purse, take it, and also a bag; and if you don't have a sword, sell your cloak and buy one." (Luke 22:35-36 NIV)

11. Zimmerman, B. 1908: The Carmelite Order. In The Catholic Encyclopedia. New York, NY: Robert Appleton

Company New Advent,
http://www.newadvent.org

As early as the times of the Prophet Samuel, there existed
in the Holy Land a body of men called Sons of the Prophets
.... With the downfall of the Kingdom of Israel, the Sons
of the Prophets disappear from history. In the third or
fourth century of the Christian Era [Mount] Carmel was
a place of pilgrimage, as is proved by numerous Greek
inscriptions on the walls of the School of the Prophets.

Chapter 3: The Essene Leader

1. The dedication of the prophet Samuel to God.

*And she made a vow, saying, "O LORD Almighty, if
you will only look upon your servant's misery and
remember me, and not forget your servant but give her
a son, then I will give him to the LORD for all the days
of his life, and no razor will ever be used on his head."
(1 Samuel 1:11 NIV)*

2. Edgar Cayce Reading 294-142; 315-4; 877-27; 1010-17;
   1151-10; 1472; 3175-3; 3344-2: Judy not only studied
   and compiled Jewish religious teachings, but also studied
   and documented Egyptian, Indian, and Persian religious
   teachings and traditions. The Persian records would
   likely have been from the Zoroastrian tradition. Many of
   the records she studied were housed in the great ancient
   library at Alexandria, Egypt, which also had a sizable

Jewish population. Her efforts to compile records from other religions were partly to understand how those recorded beliefs compared with her understanding of the Messiah and partly to preserve those ancient religious records.

3.   Edgar Cayce Reading 1151-10; 5749-15: The Apostles accepted the authority of Judy and held her in great respect for her role in administering the Essene community and teaching the young Jesus. The Jewish leaders of the other established sects, primarily the Pharisees and Sadducees, had a different opinion of Judy, possibly considering her a threat to their authority and position of power. The Roman governor and other authorities of the occupation also kept a close eye on the Essenes and the activities of its leader. Their interest was to see that no significant following arose around the Essenes that might become the nucleus of a revolt and threaten their domination of that region.

Chapter 4: The Forerunner

4.   Edgar Cayce Reading 1468-2; 5749-8: Zacharias and Elizabeth held different religious beliefs. Zacharias was not only a member of one of the major Jewish sects, likely the Pharisees, but was also part of the sect's priesthood. His wife Elizabeth was a member of the Essene community, a fact that would not have endeared her with the priests that shared Zacharias' duties. For this

reason and for her safety, Elizabeth lived in the country-side outside of Jerusalem. But the birth of John caused Zacharias to change his beliefs and accept the teaching and prophesy of the Essenes. This religious conversion cost him his life. He was murdered by his fellow priests after they became aware of his change of heart.

5. The scholarly Jerusalem Bible gives this comment as a footnote explanation for the words of Jesus concerning the murder of Zechariah.

(Matthew 23:35 and Luke 11:51) "The one referred to [Zechariah] is probably the Zechariah of 2 Ch 24:20-22. His murder is the last one to be described in the Bible (2 Ch being the last book of the Jewish Canon) while Abel's, Gn 4:8, is the first. It is possible that 'son of Barachiah' is the result of confusion with another Zechariah."

This interpretation of Jesus' words is a much less satisfying explanation than that of the readings.

6. Stevenson, Ian, 1997: Where Reincarnation and Biology Intersect: Praeger Publishers.

Chapter 5: The Mother

1. Holweck, F. 1911: Feast of the Presentation of the Blessed Virgin Mary. In The Catholic Encyclopedia. New York,

NY: Robert Appleton Company. New Advent, http://
www.newadvent.org.

2.   Edgar Cayce Reading 254-109; 649-2; 1981-1; 2603-
     1: Many more children were offered and dedicated
     to the Essene community than the twelve that were
     placed in training as a potential mother of the Messiah.
     Depending on the traits, abilities, aptitude and attitude
     of the child and with consideration for the choices of
     the child, they were trained to take on various roles
     in support of the activities of the community. In any
     large community there is a need for a cooperative effort
     among the members to ensure the daily needs of the
     community are met. The dedicated children and adults
     who entered the community on probation offered their
     lives as channels through which God might bring a new
     order and a new way of life that would change the world.
     Those who were not living at Mount Carmel, but were
     scattered throughout the larger Jewish community tried
     to bring their spiritual ideals into their daily activity.
     The training of twelve young girls who were determined
     to be the best candidates for the mother of Jesus was
     the core mission of the Essenes. These children and the
     adults who encouraged and trained them consecrated
     their lives for a greater service, to prepare a suitable
     channel through which the Son of God could find
     expression.

3. Edgar Cayce Reading 254-109; 1479-1; 5749-8: Part of
    the training of the candidates for motherhood involved
    a, perhaps daily, routine during which the girls walked
    in single file up a flight of stairs that led to an altar where
    they prayed and burned incense. The role of leader as the
    line of girls ascended the temple stairs varied from day
    to day so that each girl had an opportunity to be in front.
    On the day Mary was chosen, she was the leader.

Chapter 6: The Earthly Father

1. Edgar Cayce Reading 1602-4; 5749-8: Joseph began to
    doubt his role in the birth of the Messiah and perhaps
    the mission and purpose of the Essenes after discovering
    that Mary had become pregnant even before the wed-
    ding. He had apparently known her and had been aware
    of her ongoing training for several years but it was not
    until he went to claim his bride that he discovered she
    was pregnant. It is natural that this news would be dis-
    turbing to him and that he might be reluctant to face the
    questions and innuendos from his friends and members
    of the Essene community. It took convincing from the
    Essene leaders and direct action by God in the form of
    a visitation from an angel to allay his fears and convince
    him that all was going according to God's plan.

2. Edgar Cayce Reading 504-3; 5749-8: Joseph and Mary
    began having other children about ten years after the
    birth of Jesus. They had chosen to forego having other

children until Jesus had left their home for the teaching, care, and protection of the priests and leadership of the Essenes. This wait was a shared decision, not a requirement from God or the Essenes. The readings document two sons (James and Jude) and a daughter (Ruth) born to Mary and Joseph. After years of disbelief in the divinity of Jesus, his brother James accepts his claim and eventually becomes the leader of the church in Jerusalem. Jude [137] accepts the teachings of Jesus and writes about immorality in the early church. Ruth [1158] becomes well educated in Greece and Rome and marries a Roman citizen and supervisor of tax collection by the name of Philoas [1151].

Chapter 7: The Immaculate Conception

1. Stevenson, Ian, 2000: Children Who Remember Previous Lives: A Question of Reincarnation: McFarland and Company Inc.

2. Kirkpatrick, Sidney, 2016: *The Remarkable Story of Cayce Jones*; Venture Inward, March 2016, volume 32, number 1, page 4.

3. Edgar Cayce Reading 263-13; 282-3; 2072-8: Souls are attracted to and chose their future parents based on personal relationships that need to be resolved or continued, the genetic heritage of the new-born infant and the earthly environment it will experience during

its early years. The ideals and purposes of the parents during the conception of the future infant are important considerations for the incoming soul. Despite the many considerations, the choice to inhabit the infant is made by the soul and it is responsible for that body, after it has grown and developed in physical consciousness to the point where it begins to express itself and manifests its own purposes and desires.

4. Edgar Cayce Reading 457-10; 2390-2: A soul may monitor the progress of a growing infant before it is born, but the actual entry of the soul into the infant and its earthly environment is roughly correlated with the physical birth of the infant. This incarnation can occur as early as the first physical breath of the infant or as late as twenty four hours after the first breath, and occasionally within a few hours before birth. The soul may even change its mind, allowing another soul to take possession of the body. It makes sense that the soul entry occurs near or shortly after the birth, because if the soul enters a developing infant before it is separated from the mother at birth, two souls would be competing for expression in the same body.

Chapter 8: The Inn and the Birth

1. Edgar Cayce Reading 262-103; 1152-3; 5749-15: It was late evening when the group of travelers arrived at the inn and they must have been tired. They all were

disappointed when Apsafar, the innkeeper and a member of the Essenes, appeared at the door and pronounced that there were no rooms available. At first, neither Joseph nor Mary, nor their traveling companions realized the reason for the rejection and refusal to allow the group into the inn. Apsafar was actually protecting Joseph and Mary from the rabble that had collected at the inn to participate in the Roman census. He steered them away from the crowded inn toward the safety of the stable which had already been prepared for them. The Bible casts him as a villain because he refused to give Joseph and Mary a room and does not give him the credit he deserves for his concern and foresight.

GENERAL NOTES

1. The Edgar Cayce readings are housed at the Association for Research and Enlightenment located in Virginia Beach, Virginia. The A.R.E. not only archives the readings and associated correspondence to and from the people who requested readings, but also engages in publishing, teaching and exploring the concepts presented in the readings. Topics of investigation include holistic health, meditation and prayer, spirituality and the relationship of man and God, dream interpretation and intuition, psychic phenomena, and reincarnation. Many of the readings offer insights into mankind's ancient history and long struggle to find its way back to God.

2. References to the Edgar Cayce readings are denoted by a sequence of (usually) two digits. For example, the number 5749-8 refers to reading number 5749 (a number assigned to the person for whom the reading was conducted to ensure anonymity) and the eighth reading in a series of readings for that person. A single digit reference refers to all readings for the person assigned that number.

3. For an excellent summary of Essene references in ancient documents consult the International Standard

Bible Encyclopedia Online website: www.internation-alstandardbible.com/E/essenes.html

4. Krajenke, Robert W., 2012, Edgar Cayce's Story of the Bible, A.R.E. Press.

The Old Testament records the creation of the universe and the earth it contains, the creation of Adam and Eve and their loss of God consciousness and separation from their creator, and the rise and struggles of the nation of Israel as it alternately seeks and abandons God. These Old Testament stories are brought to life again and made more personal in this book that combines the Bible, the readings of several dozens of persons who were told by Edgar Cayce that they had incarnated during Old Testament times, and the biblical insights of Edgar Cayce through transcribed records of his Tuesday Night Bible Class.

5. Furst, Jeffrey, 1976, Edgar Cayce's Story of Jesus, Berkley Books.

This comprehensive book describes the incarnations and activities of many individuals recounted through the Edgar Cayce readings, focusing on those who lived in ancient Egypt and Persia, and who lived in Palestine during the life of Jesus and the struggles of the early Christian church. Many of these people were active participants in the Essene community and were among those who were preparing for the expected birth of the Messiah, and knew Jesus during his life and ministry. It explores their daily activities, doubts, and triumphs as they tried to understand and process the historic events which were unfolding around them. The lives of some well-known biblical figures are developed in greater detail and several important historical figures not mentioned in the Bible are brought to life.